Strengthening

the Spiritual Life

Strengthening
the Spiritual Life

by

Nels F. S. Ferré

Professor of Philosophical Theology
Vanderbilt University School of Religion

Harper & Brothers Publishers New York

STRENGTHENING THE SPIRITUAL LIFE

To My Sisters

Thyra Bjorn

Margaret Ferré

Ann Whitaker

Karin Herr

faithful co-workers in the
life of the Spirit

Contents

Preface

THE content of this book was delivered to the International Convention of Disciples of Christ. Through the courtesy of its executive secretary, Dr. Gaines M. Cook, these addresses are now offered to the general public.

I am deeply indebted to my wife and to Miss Marilynn Hindman for their constant co-operation during the writing of this book both in typing and in stylistic improvements. At this time, too, I want to acknowledge the warm feeling of gratitude I have toward all the members in the Religious Book Department of Harper & Brothers.

NELS F. S. FERRÉ

Nashville, Tennessee
September 11, 1950

Strengthening

the Spiritual Life

I

A Formula for Spiritual Success

"I HAVE come to the seminary to learn to pray," said "Mother Alice" Kahokuoluna of the Kalaupapa Leper Colony speaking in chapel. "That is my biggest need as I face my situation." Deep in the pew I felt very small, knowing that we seminary professors could teach other things far better than we could teach that.

"Before the missionaries came to Hawaii," she went on in effect, "my people used to sit outside their temples for a long time meditating and preparing themselves before entering. Then they would virtually creep to the altar to offer their petition and afterward would again sit a long time outside, this time to 'breathe life' into their prayers. The Christians, when they came, just got up, uttered a few sentences, said Amen and were done. For that reason my people called them haolis, 'without breath,' or those who fail to breathe life into their prayers."

Many of us feel today that the greatest challenge is to breathe vitality into our spiritual life. Unless our life of the spirit is strengthened we have no real hope. With it strengthened, we and our children can see an age fulfilling the hopes we hardly dare cherish.

Our times need religion, not because nothing else is left, but because there is nothing better. Social confusion, political insecurity, and military destruction beset us on every hand. The church that was born to bless stands pretty much with empty hands. It has lost heart. What voice it has gives utterance to the ways of the world. The church speaks too often with the wisdom of *Time* magazine and the realism of newspaper and radio.

Most people are anxious. They worry. Little children, supposedly sheltered in Christian homes, have nightmares and wake up screaming that the Russians are coming. Even good Christian folk are doubting their faith. They wonder if its assurance is not garnish for a poisoned platter. They have come to suspect that the main dish is always bitter and fatal, religion with its trimmings being therefore a disguise of the true facts. Our age is sick of idealism and spews it out as a deceit.

Yet deep in their insides these same people have a lingering awareness of the realism of religion at its authentic best. They always did know that an easy religion is a false promise. True faith makes radical demands and commands radical treatments. Within their heart of hearts they are on the way to understanding that God's will for the common good is no sentimental idealism, but concrete living; that it alone can save us from our social confusion, our political insecurity, and our military annihilation.

Many times God speaks through dreams to those attentive to His voice. One night recently my wife dreamt that she was back in a college classroom with the assignment of an English theme on "How to Stop Worrying." As she sat gazing at the sheet of paper, wondering where to begin, she felt impelled to compose rapidly, in a hand not her own, a flow of inspired words. Upon awaking, she could remember only the three points of the outline: Worship, work, wait. I should like to prescribe this "divine formula" for all who need relief from worry, rest from work, and peace of heart for genuine well-being.

Worship is the baring of one's whole life unto God. Ritual is not worship. Worship is the finding and the acceptance of the real. Whatever the means used, worship is the soul's intercourse with God. Worship is not only the occasional standing on holy ground but the constant living on it. Worship comes from knowing what life is all about. Worship follows seeing and feeling beyond the fleeting moment. To worship is to be gripped by God. Worship—provided it is the worship of the true God—is the living in and by eternity. To worship aright is being invaded by the deathless freshness of eternal love and everlasting life. Such worship reveals life as it is and God as He is, and by the seeing of Him conquers every anxiety. This vision of God is a prescription for true peace and power and the cure for all worry.

Worship issues in adoration. One day after I had been weeks in pain to the point of utter discouragement, my Christian mother overheard me praying, "Dear Lord, if thou wilt ever have me well and use me again, thy will be done; if not, thy will be done anyway." "Nels," she reproved, "that's no way to pray. Thank Him and praise Him; thank Him and praise Him." This I did; then I better understood what adoration meant. God's will is constantly for the best, whatever happens. Come what may, He is to be thanked and praised.

Either we co-operate with Him or we do not. If we co-operate, He blesses us with His presence, whether we feel it or not. We get the chance to turn all suffering, loss, and limitation into the glorying in afflictions, the possession of nothing that makes us rich, the opportunity for healing faith and helping service. If this health and these open doors become ours, moreover, they become the means for good works and these, when others see them, cause them to praise our Father in heaven.

If, on the contrary, we fail to accept God's will for our good, our refusal finally thwarts us. He will not let us keep going forever our own foolish way. He makes the road ahead rough and threatening. Yet He is continually stretching out His arms to save us for His better way.

The sovereign Lord is saving love. To accept Him is to adore Him. To lack gratitude and joy is a failure to see and to accept the true and living God. Perfect love casts out fear. The worship of God is the end of worry. While we worship we cannot worry. But as long as we worry we cannot worship.

To worship God is to know that whatever happens is for the best. To be sure, our sin and foolishness are not good, but that we be both free and have a chance to learn is for the best. The depth of our trouble measures the strength of our freedom and the height of God's grace. Since God is sovereign love, all things work together for good to those who love Him. This good is the coming of His kingdom with power and speed. The more we love Him and the more we are who do love Him, the mightier and faster is the coming of His kingdom. When our hearts are in heaven we find our treasures in the doing and spreading of God's will among men.

This working together for good may seem anything but good to the unbeliever and the misunderstander. It may mean a cross, a crucifying of self and of all the self's works. But the worshiper glories in the cross where bane or blessing is sanctified. True, he never seeks the cross, but he is always willing to take it up and to bear it. The worshiper accepts both the cross and the crown with adoring acquiescence. While looking one night for a Scripture verse for meditation I happened to turn to a text promising that he who trusts God shall never be disappointed. My wife's comment was that most people would probably construe this to mean that everything would go well with them, humanly speaking! How much deeper lies the truth that he who lives in worship understands that God's ways are always best and that in accepting them he lives in adoration.

Worship also helps us see ourselves as we are and to see things as they are. What is stranger than ourselves? We know that hair turns gray, but how personal gray hair looks on ourselves! We know that people grow old and die, but how strange for *us* to have children in college or to have grandchildren. And how strange to face the inevitable end of this life. Perhaps stranger to some is to see themselves sinning, to feel themselves loved, to know themselves forgiven and in the presence of God. Most of the time, however, we are strangers to ourselves.

Nor can we even measure ourselves correctly. We hide from ourselves the parts which we do not like. We paint over such elements to make them seem strong and pretty; this we do with our eyes closed lest we should see ourselves as we are. We do not dare to face ourselves, for all our trying to change ourselves has failed. Only when we worship the living God do we dare accept ourselves as we are in the light and judgment of what we ought to be. For when we worship Him there is hope of forgiveness and promise of a new life. He sends forth judgment unto victory. Whatsoever is born of God overcomes the world.

To worship aright is not only to see ourselves but also to see things more clearly as they are. Public opinion is always being declared by neighbors, clubs, pulpit, press, movies, and radio. Commentators become professionally excited over every event. We feel lost in the tangle of propaganda emitted by interest groups. Only as we gain the perspective and proportion of God's work in history do we see what really is happening. Then we stand amazed at the unreality and false tensions of the world. Disasters bespeak God's constant judgment and prove His faithfulness. The deepest threats to our existence are the scales that weigh our aims. The victories of the world are scaled down to size. Small signs of the Spirit thunder their ultimate importance.

The pace of God, too, tests our own pace. His long-suffering purposes our salvation, and only as we know for certain in our hearts that love never fails and can never lose its own can we find the eternal relaxation which achieves the maximum through creative concern. Worship is the first and the pre-eminent prescription for worry. Worship is the finding of peace and power, for it is the living in the presence of God.

The second part of the formula on how to stop worrying was work. Only he who worships can labor to the fullest advantage, for all work is ordained by God for our true good. God gives us work to do because He shares with us His own creativeness. Jesus knew that his Father worked as well as he. The Sabbath symbolizes His day of rest, but the seventh day precedes six days of work. The rest of God in fellowship, pure and full, is the climax of reality, but such rest follows and is dependent upon, to all eternity, six days of creative work. This ratio of work to rest is the proportion established by God's experience. We, too, as His children need the same proportion in our lives, if they are to find the purer and fuller rest of fellowship as a sabbath enjoyment.

Worry ceases when we work with God, for His work always counts. To work within His purpose for the common good is to find and to feel life's real meaning. Such work is the surest cure for the despair of futility. It gives zest to life because it helps human needs. No work is real unless it does. It also inspires us with the sense of victory, for God's work never fails. We know that we do God's work when we truly strive for the common good, not as pleasers of men but unto God.

Many work to "get ahead," which means to get themselves ahead. They find no escape from anxiety. They grow old swiftly, in spirit and in body, and even acquire headaches, nervousness, stomach ulcers and insomnia. He who cannot sleep because of a cup of coffee ought to examine his purpose in the struggle. Perhaps this turns out to be personal ambition—to receive glory from others and not the true glory of God. Others work to get money for pleasure, for display, or for security. They get no relief from anxiety. They know what worry means, but they fail to understand or to make use of the Bible's advice to take pleasure in their exertions.

Still others escape life in work. They think that while they are buried in work they are immune to worry. But they are not. Far from it. While their hands are busy their minds are busy too. Their temper grows short; their mood grows dark; their body shows the strain. No one can hide from God, no one can flee from others or even from himself, no matter how thick the barricade of work.

Work in itself, merely as activity, cannot satisfy the person's sense of meaning and of importance. When toil is solely a means and is not regarded as a medium of fellowship with God and men, people so engaged bend and twist their very natures and natural interests. But those who cannot enjoy the day or sleep at night soon lose the capacity to enjoy pleasure, esteem, or power. They are to be pitied who do not make a melody within their heart out of their work.

Those who work with a single heart unto God find joy and strength and pleasure in their efforts. Even those who are not allowed to do what they crave can hear in the prison of circumstance a midnight song of deliverance. For working unto God always constitutes a light burden and an easy yoke. When work is worship God transfigures every task with His own presence, and the pay envelope occasions no protest. The New Testament can teach us this. Some speak of that book as reactionary, that it accepts the status quo, even slavery. How much deeper is its message. Personal attitudes in work and social relations will both be transformed, not through coercives of legislation nor even through social pressure, but mainly through an indwelling grace which transforms every circumstance and every relation, the master and the slave becoming brothers of each other in the Lord. Christianity does not mean the doing away with legitimately different economic functions. These are necessary to organized industry. But Christianity brings true democracy and the true sharing of the products of labor because of its spirit of common concern under God with whom there is no respect of person. A pity it is that most people consider this spiritual and social democracy as merely a beautiful theory. Nothing can more surely bring in the classless and raceless society as a real attitude than the Christian faith in actual practice.

Worship is man's most important work. To work is to direct

one's efforts according to some purpose. We need play, too, purposeless effort for fun and relaxation. We need to have, even more, effortless fellowship. But real worship, correctly understood and pursued, is hard work. Through prayer, witness, and work we direct our lives to its central aim of loving God and making Him more loved by all people.

The preacher has no monopoly here. As long as the church witness is a solo rather than a chorus it is going to lack depth and volume. You cannot make the minister into a prima donna and expect a strong church. Only when all the members really unite at worshiping God with their whole life can the world become transformed by the power of the Gospel. Farmers, doctors, carpenters, lawyers, housewives, teachers, cattlemen—all must practice to sing the new song of our common humanity unto the Lord of creative power. When worship becomes generally a steady job, and work our steady worship, the world shall see life assuming a new quality, a new you, a new peace, an absence of anxiety that shall make it take note and take heart. If we want to stop worrying we must make our work into worship and our worship into work so that the peak attainment of the six days of work may be reached in the pure fellowship of the seventh day of worship, and rest in God and with God.

The third article of the divine prescription against worry was wait. To wait is not easy. It is a hard lesson to learn. In patience we are promised to possess our souls, but how few of us succeed. Our capacity for waiting shows our concrete trust in God. God's way is not our way and God's pace is not ours. The less we are willing to wait the less we believe Him. Anxiety shows itself to a great extent in restlessness. People cannot even allow the muscles of their faces or their hands to relax. Worriers rub their hands, wash their hands, fiddle with their rings or watch chains, thump cigarettes, or dawdle with anything that is handy. They must ever be doing something. They do not like to be still even in church. Prolonged silence makes them nervous. Something must happen, and if they are not causing it, they are sure that nothing is happening.

On this subject I can speak from experience. As a child I was extremely high-strung. On school days I wanted to be wakened far too early and would run all the way to school as if the devil were after me. My father could not bear to wait for people. My mother dreaded keeping him waiting when he was going somewhere. Ever since childhood, too, I have had to fight a drive that rebelled against waiting. But God knew the cure. All my life I have had to wait abnormally long for many things which I wanted in a particular hurry. The fever of life made me fret and fume on such occasions; and often I must have been hard on those who had to wait with me. Such real victory as I have experienced—and it is genuine and by no means petty—has come through prayer and total surrender to God's will. Most of the hurry was self-will and not concern for others; it was a trusting of myself rather than of God.

Some people cannot trust themselves enough to believe that what is done well and with a good intention can be let go. They are always berating themselves for what they did or did not do and stewing over the results. They cannot wait to grow themselves and to see their work ripen. Nor can they wait to be corrected by time. They must be perfect and above blame right away. They therefore picture themselves and their work in a false light and sputter when they are not recognized or their deeds are not appreciated.

Nor can they trust others. They cannot delegate responsibility. Unless they do the thing themselves they feel that nothing will be done right; at least they cannot wait and see. Nor can they wait to let others grow. They do things for their children to get them done properly. Then they worry because they have not time for everything, because they get no rest, because their children do not mature and assume responsibility, because everyone considers them bossy and prefers for fellowship others who do not "amount to" so much as they. The world can do little with these self-serious perfectionists. They cannot know fellowship, for they trust only themselves. Other people are unreal and they cannot take time for them to show what they can do, what responsibility they can shoulder, or what capacity for growth is in them.

Harder still is it to wait for God. His patience seems slackness. After all, He has eternity and our concern is present time. The world is wrong and we are here to right it, and at once. The zeal of many a reformer is disguised atheism. Much desire to please others is nervous self-protection. What God wants, however, is relaxed, trustful waiting.

Obviously not all waiting is good. Some escape life into spiritlessness. They have no energy because they dare not face life. They are tired and suffer from low blood pressure because of worry. Both high and low blood pressure, both stomach ulcers and lack of appetite may be signs of worry and of a lingering death. Some people dread making decisions and put off action as long as possible. Some have their security in things as they are and would wait forever before attempting anything new. Waiting may be the result of laziness or indifference. Certainly we must not exalt waiting into the essence of faith.

Nevertheless experience does work patience, when experience is itself worked over in worship. Real waiting is concerned waiting. It is more than interested watching. It is feeling and knowing oneself involved in the outcome. It is being personally invested in the result. It is love's being with and for those who must do the deciding for themselves. Real waiting is also expectant waiting. Love never fails. Christian concern hopes all things. It is continually on the edge of seeing things happen. Christian waiting finds things done according to its faith. It may find open results and rejoice. It may find the patience of unanswered prayer and rejoice. It is never wearied in well-doing when that well-doing is misinterpreted or rejected. Christian waiting witnesses in season and out of season. Fainting not, it reaps in due time. When that time is due God knows, and His blessing is always on time.

Real waiting is also victorious waiting. We have unsolvable problems, but God has none. We have permanent problem children, but He does not. We die and do not see the fruits of our labor in this life, but God never dies and beyond this life we shall see the reward of every deed done in the body. Real waiting is victorious waiting because though our warfare seems constant the outcome is certain.

Those who are on God's side never know final defeat. They cannot feel sorry for themselves because they are edged out of positions of influence, because they are kept from leadership, because even their motives are stigmatized. They bear on their body only the stigmas of their Lord and they witness to the power of the sons of the resurrection. Real waiting is living within the quiet joy and peace of God's own way, more natural than the return of the salmon to its breeding place or of the waterfowl to its summer nest. Such waiting is the cure for worry, for it is living within the perspective, pace, and proportion of God. Such waiting is peace and power.

Real waiting is the soul's sabbath rest amidst the unrest and confusion of the workaday world.

This, then, is the divine prescription against worry; this is the divine cure of anxiety; this is the divine healing for spirit, mind, and body: Worship, work, wait. We turn now to consider more concretely ways of personal, family, and group devotions, with the confidence that anyone who faithfully follows this prescription cannot only stop worrying but also find, surprisingly, peace of mind, peace of soul, and the peace of God which passes all understanding.

II

Strengthening Through Personal Devotions

PRAYER is man's most accessible means to the greatest possible power. Not only can we bring about a whole new world through prayer but one's own life can by its means become astonishingly new. The sick, the crippled, the shut-in, and the imprisoned can pray with the same power as can the strong man and the influential woman. The child is heard by God as are the aged and the dying. Although prayer is everywhere available it is nevertheless almost universally wasted and neglected. What can be more important, therefore, than that each one of us learn to use better this great gift of God?

We are not going to argue about the reality and power of prayer. The giants of religion have been men of prayer; they were not great for themselves but for the world, thereby changing the world, as well as themselves, for the better. "The saints who changed the world" is no mere phrase; they were history's most real people. Instead of arguing about them we must take up their task. This we cannot do, however, apart from prayer. No one can improve the world drastically and with such speed as is now needed except God; and He, respecting our freedom, will not do so apart from our co-operation. Our fullest co-operation can come only through the community of prayer. We all need to learn to pray better; this is life's most important lesson.

Only by praying can this lesson be learned. There is no way to acquiring skill except by doing. Theoretically a man may study to throw ringers in horseshoes; actually to throw them he must practice for the peg. Many truths about prayer can be explored through theory but no learning will become personal experience and reality apart from the doing. Every skill takes time and patience, but the reality of prayer, being life's chief lesson, is therefore also its hardest. Prayer as communion with God, the center of life, can never be mastered easily. The very difficulty shows its importance and reality. Yet it is a lesson which all must learn sooner or later, in this life or beyond, for the career of one's soul itself is measured by it. Every other attainment is ultimately for the sake of this one, making prayer for the wise person the primary aim of his life. Our knowing and loving God, our concern for the world, our personal fulfillment and satisfaction—all are drawn together in the reality and progress of our prayer life. Prayer, then, is first on life's agenda and no one can afford to be unconcerned about it.

Now, I want to share with you a few hints from my personal experience as to how the practice of prayer may be improved. The first rule we all need to learn is relaxation. We cannot come into the divine presence tense and terse and expect to meet the divine. In this state of tension we are still very much involved in ourselves. We have to let go. Such letting go is true of life as a whole. A report has it that a large sum was spent in teaching Ted Williams to relax at the batter's plate. A golfer will shoot fairly well until he is obsessed to do better. Then he usually becomes tense and does far worse! God has made the world self-defeating for the self-serious! Relaxation is needed in prayer as in everything else.

How can this be accomplished? Each person, naturally, must find his own best way. There is no substitute for personal experience. It is better, nevertheless, to lie in bed while praying in order to relax than to kneel in stiff discomfort on a stone floor. There are moods, to be sure, when falling on one's knees or stretching out one's arms while standing are entirely appropriate. My own deepest experience, for instance, came while kneeling in my customary prayer corner. But for long sustained prayer the body should be at ease. Jesus may have prayed sitting on a ledge or a hillside through early morning hours. Comfortable sitting or lying I believe to be important aids to relaxed prayer. The many years I had to pray while sick in bed taught me this lesson.

There are also concrete aids to relaxation. One such aid is literally to take one's whole self and place it in God's hands, saying: "Holy Spirit, take me as I am and do thou help me to pray. Here I put myself in thy hands completely. Receive me completely, both my willing and my unwilling parts." In my own case I feel physical surrender starting to overspread me from above my eyebrows. Conscious relaxation of wrists, ankles, and neck also help in the physical preparation.

For a reason unknown to me I have also found that a surrendered, steady upward turning of my closed eyes has not only unbound me, but released in me some creative flow that causes the whole body to flush with a sense of well-being. Something of the same effect is had when, in imagination, I let my whole self sink back as though my head were being lowered on an uptilted cot. These techniques are physically effective to the point that I have long hesitated to use or to mention them, for in theory, wanting pure spirituality, I have been afraid of any bodily approach, and certainly of every technique. I have wondered where this creative surge would take me. The more I have prayed, however, the more I have discovered how God uses such means; the actual result has been health and creative zest, a happy family, and many more open doors in my work. I have therefore decided to give God the glory by the sharing of these experiences for what they may be worth to other seekers. In any case, bodily relaxation I believe to be of utmost importance for effective prayer.

Along with relaxation comes recollection. The order here is not fixed. Genuineness and naturalness are most important. Discipline is good and some order is necessary to steady growth, but order can become a rut and discipline a mere habit. Sometimes we wake up practically with a shout of glory, knowing ourselves to be in God's presence and suffused with adoration and joy. The more fully prayer possesses the heart, the longer, the more natural is such experience of immediate adoration. But for most beginners there is prior need of willed relaxation and recollection.

Recollection involves first of all the recalling of who God is. God is sovereign love. He is both ultimate reality and our most intimate friend. We should not pray as pagans, bowing and scraping or pleading to be heard. God is more real and near than we are and wants to have fellowship with us far more than we want it with Him. *To be able to remember who God is, is perhaps the hardest prerequisite of true prayer.* We tend to treat God as though He were one of us. We endow Him with our own love of glory, desire for revenge, or hardness of heart. Either that or He is not real to us and we try to make Him real by dint of much fervor and hard praying. We keep forgetting that if we will but call on Him honestly, He hears and helps us more than we can ask or think.

The second thing to recollect is that God loves everyone completely. Somehow or other it is hard not to think of oneself as a favorite child. We want to get something from God for ourselves alone. Much of such praying hurts us and we should be better off not praying at all. By praying in that way we get even more wrapped up in ourselves and farther away from God. Instead we should always recall that God is always completely for all, and that we cannot pray to Him aright unless we are completely surrendered to the common good. Our answered prayer may, in fact, be a cross borne for the common welfare. Or our best blessing may be given to us precisely in order for us to give it to others.

Only within this view of God ought we to remember how He also cares completely for us and how we can take to Him our every care and problem. Sometimes we try to play God by practicing love to all without recognizing how deeply we most of all need God Himself and His care if we are to be enabled to bless others and humble enough to be blessed by them.

Conscious relaxation keeps us from rushing thoughtlessly into the holy presence. Recollection makes us recall with whom we have dealing. God is completely ready to forgive and He never holds a thing against us, as might an offended human being. He grieves rather over the fact that we will not trust His love enough to forsake those ways which keep us from Him. Knowing that He longs to forgive and to restore us in order that we might walk in the newness of life, we must therefore lift up our lives to be restored by His faithfulness.

We do not realize our own deepest need for restoration. Because sin has clouded our vision we see ourselves mostly as good. Therefore we defend ourselves from the hurt of failure and from the sting of guilt. But prayer restores the Publican who knows he is a sinner, and leaves Pharisee unchanged who is conscious of his good deeds. If we feel no need for restoration we are very likely self-righteous. When our guilt becomes unbearable we may develop into a self-righteousness which is a form of mental illness. Some fanatical leaders, for instance, are very prone to think that they are God's anointed while they are closer to being candidates for the asylum. Forms of the Christian faith which stress sinlessness are particularly tempted in this respect. All of us, however, need constantly to pray for forgiveness and the restoring of the joy of our salvation.

Prayer is communion. At times it consists in talking with God. But much communion ought to be spent in silence. Happy lovers know the depth of wordless fellowship. Constant jabbering wearies. The more we know and love God the more we ought to practice wordless prayers. In the deepest moments of their lives men are struck dumb and numb not only with sorrow but with deep joy. Since prayer is fellowship we ought to insure quietness in order to listen. How otherwise are we to hear? God does not speak with certainty to those who cannot hear the still small voice.

Yet, deeper than the silence of listening is the silence of communion. Mystics have called this union, rather than communion. But the merger of spirits is no merger of personalities. Beyond the abstractive powers of consciousness and the strains of personal individuality, oneness in holy communion is a high and holy reality. Though I am here putting silence early in the period of prayer, profound silence, where the soul is bathed in the love of God through wordless surrender and communion, should occur intermittently throughout any prolonged experience of it.

Generally prayer is supposed to begin with adoration. For full-fledged saints this is very likely the practice. Sometimes many also wake with such joy or go apart to pray with such exultation that nothing but the pure adoration of God seems to matter. Other times we need preparation of spirit, however, before we can genuinely adore God. When we really know who God is and trust that all is eventually for the best, however, we cannot help adoring Him. Adoration cannot be forced. Adoration is the self's finding reality and rest. Adoration is the vision of God and feeling the fruition of His love. Adoration is the soul's sabbath experience, as whoever has tasted it knows. Anyone who was ever raised to the seventh heaven in or out of the body understands this "fragment of the future."

Gratitude follows adoration as night the day. We praise God for Himself, for His love and even our own blessings are acknowledged in humble thanksgiving. Life is new and rich and hopes abound unto thanksgiving. Within this exultant gratitude the longing steals to bless others and to serve. Thus intercession and petition for service begin to pour out along with the thanksgiving. No neat boundaries can be drawn for the rich prayer life. Adoration, thanksgiving, love, the desire to bless, the urge to be better, the will to please God and to help others, all interweave, then stream off into separate strands only to flow together in some other channel.

When we pray, however, we have the right to examine the spirit. We may often speak with spontaneous tongues, but in general there ought to be decency and order even in personal prayer life. The content of our prayer life ought to revolve around two focal points: We need to pray both from God's perspective and from our own. The Lord's Prayer is a perfect illustration of this truth. If we really adore and love God, we must try to see everything from His point of view. When doing so, we rejoice in God's eternity, in His eternal creations beyond our knowing, in His sure saving of all men in His time and way. Then we live in glory with the saints who have prepared the way. Jesus, "the forerunner," becomes the pioneer of our own faith.

Then all religions can be surveyed as man's seeking after God and God's letting himself be known at divers times and places. All questings become strangely dear, while in the same insight an urge to show the full love of God in Christ becomes our constant concern. Somehow, when God's perspective is accepted we behold our true transiency within the vast processes of God's eternity; but we see also the endless meaning of our lives within the purposes of God. We may find an aid in steadfastly imagining God's eyes looking down, down with love to all men, waiting for us to do our part. And His hand rests on our shoulder as we keep repeating "Lord here am I; use me."

We need also to pray from our own point of view, not selfishly, of course, but from the station where God has put us and from which He can use us and us alone. This place is our locus of responsibility and our chance to bless. Thus we offer up our own lives to God's service, come what may. We ask Him to do anything He pleases with us, to deliver us from all self-concern, to free us from prejudice and smallness of heart, to mingle our lives with the hosts of God who work trustfully for the coming of His Kingdom. We may then lift up our families, member by member, examining our own failures in relation to them, asking for concrete concern and actual thoughtfulness, and beyond that for our Father's richest blessing on their lives. We cannot pray for their external welfare and success, but that God's full will be done in each one of them, that He may be real to them, and that life's best blessings may come to them in whatever form God wants to give it. We may after that enter into our own gift of ancestry, thanking God for our forebears, generations back, and asking that we be worthy of their legacy, even increasing their faithfulness.

Then we may naturally branch out into the needs of relatives beyond the immediate family, close friends, and particularly into the necessities of those who are on our special list. Over the years we meet those who ask for our prayers or who become our particular charges. We may go on to bless our local church, the various churches, the Church Universal and its leaders. We may pray for different branches of faith—Roman Catholic, Greek Orthodox, Lutheran, Episcopal, Baptist, Mennonite, Brethren, Seventh Day Adventist, Christian Scientist, Moravian, Methodist, Presbyterian, Friends, Congregationalist and others, sometimes for some and sometimes for others. Or we may intercede for institutions which train the clergy, particularly the teachers of the ministry. They need such prayer incalculably.

We may pray, also, for missionaries, now in one country then in another, or for people we know all over the world. Or we may pray for community leaders, teachers, labor leaders, leaders of business or professions, housewives, college students, patients in hospitals, convicts in prison, for our country, for so-called enemy countries, for the United Nations. There seems to be no end to the objects of our petitions, and the more we pray the more we have to keep selecting items for special stress. Somehow, too, all of life comes closer and we sense our belonging to all God's creatures as we pray for them and love them with God's concern. Very likely we end our prayer with thanksgiving and by committing all things into God's care and keeping. Best of all is the closing of prayer with silent communion.

Amid the hustle and bustle, however, where there never is time enough for what we have to do, how can there possibly be time for such praying? Preachers may find it, but can a layman? During years of sickness when I could not sleep for pain, I discovered the joy and strength of praying at night. Like the monks who used to get up various times during the night to worship God, I would lie back letting myself sink into God. Too weary to struggle, throwing my spent self on the Holy Spirit, I experienced real rest and an unmistakable inflow of power. My body began to flush with new life. Much sleeping is "for sorrow." It is due to tension and is an escape from trouble. When all is surrendered, the spirit, body, and mind find such rest in prayer that instead of having less energy a new creative force emerges. Of late years I have discovered the possibilities of early morning. Jesus himself knew this secret and used it. Even a married man whose early rising would wake his wife and children can nevertheless lie reverently in bed and pray through the early morning hours. A specific time need not be set, for God wakes His own lovers early enough for the purpose.

Another valuable prayer time is just before work. Prayer starts the work right. But everybody must find his own time and method. A farmer can pray on the tractor; a housewife, while doing dishes, or while ironing. Instead of listening to the radio or reading the newspaper one can listen to God and meditate on high matters. Prayer brings relaxation and rest after a hard day. A girl in love always finds time to think of her lover regardless of how busy she is. Anyone who loves God finds ample time to share God's concern each day. A particularly good opportunity for praying is afforded by traveling on trains or on buses, or while driving a car.

Prayer should provide the constant set of the self. As soon as the spirit is freed from concentration on work or on company, one rises to God in praise and holy communion. When we think of friends or meet people, the heart jumps up to bless them without them knowing it. When we enter a new city we bless it. When we read a new book we bless its writer and its reading. When we hear a speaker we cannot help exalting him to be used by God, and we pray that our own lives may be readied for the fullest response.

Made inwardly rich through constant prayer, we may begin to hear almost constant voices. How shall we treat these voices? First, let us be thankful for them. Prayer is conversation and the spirit speaks in quiet and real communion with those who cultivate such prayer. Secondly, we shall test them by the simple method of lifting them up to the Holy Spirit, saying in effect, "I can't know for certain if this be thy voice; O Lord, do thou show me more plainly. Particularly deliver me from subtly suggesting my own will." If the voice persists and is in line with God's concern for the common good, we can accept it and act upon it. God can use autosuggestion, if acceptance be that. If the voices prove sometimes mistaken, that should not make an end to praying. Trust God and go on to victory.

After years of hearing such voices a pattern of answer will become compellingly real, including perhaps astonishing predictions or actual healings. One should avoid talk about these voices, however, and not depend upon them as final authorities. Rejoice, rather, that God is faithful. Fellowship is far more important than power to know or to do. By all means refrain from making the rule that the voice must go against the inclinations. Such promptings may be due to fear or to the will to die. *Rather, test the voices thankfully and believingly according to God's concern for the common good.* Let every blessing bless and let God abound to you and through you.

Again, to depend upon feelings is dangerous. You may learn after a while that when you feel weakest God is doing the most through you. Did not even Jesus feel that he could do nothing in himself? When God seems almost absent to you, someone else may find God compellingly real through your life. The closer you live to God, however, the more should hope abound and joy flood your soul. You should learn to rejoice always. If such joy is not a common occurrence you are not praying right. Our faith is a Gospel. Perhaps you need to learn the lesson of simplicity, to trust God as a small child trusts his father. The Christian also stops pretending. He becomes open and simple. Sophistication is the wisdom of the wise, and this is foolishness to God. By simple trust in God's absolute love your feelings become genuinely positive; and the more you trust, the more you will find both the inner peace and the outer poise you seek.

Finally, give God glory without show. Avoid unnatural piety.

Jesus told us to anoint our faces so that people will not see that we fast, and to pray in the inner closet. Nevertheless, your light is not to be hid under a bushel or a bed. Live openly, though humbly, the power of the Gospel. Let your life testify to God's grace. If He has healed you, proclaim thankfully His praise. If He has prospered you, never claim for yourself the power to cause growth or to give increase. If He has put you in the shadow, dwell there in order to bear witness to the power of light to overcome it. If you face failure and death, testify through both to God's total victory.

God is concerned to use your life. May your prayer life be so relaxed and so filled with recollection, that you may feel the joy of your salvation restored through forgiveness, and in silent adoration thank Him. Thus by lifting up His Kingdom and all your own concerns under Him, you may steadily hear His voice of warning or of approval and may feel Him so real and near that others will testify to the Gospel of the grace of God declared in your life. Each one of us can improve his own prayer life; the exact way must be discovered by every individual until he knows the Spirit's manner of working. But for each one of us there is waiting an ever fuller satisfaction and usefulness of life through prayer.

III

Strengthening Through Family
Devotions

Win the family for Christian living and the world is won. The family is the seat of our basic troubles and the source of our noblest hopes. This claim is no mere theory. This is factual truth.

We now know how deeply children are affected by their homes. For a while some psychologists went to extremes, teaching that children are permanently formed in infancy. This is not true. Human nature is plastic and continually open to change. It is most plastic, however, in early childhood; and character is more basically set there than some like to think. Our parents do not stop disciplining us when the physical action of spanking stops nor do they cease spoiling us when we leave home. Their dispositions, right or wrong, become formative conditions of our lives with which we have to contend as long as we live.

The fruit seldom falls far from the tree. Sometimes it is carried elsewhere by extraneous forces. Not only apples but children are picked up and planted, for good or for ill, in alien soil. No parent should therefore judge himself completely responsible for the conduct of a wayward child nor must he boast too personally of a successful offspring. There is real freedom for the child, and other influences than parental ones help make him what he is. But for the most part the fruit falls near by. Children are usually mirrors in whom parents can see reflected their own images. For this reason, because of their own guilt, the older generation tends to be either too hard or too easy on its successor.

Jesus grasped the right formula for a new life. "Make the tree good." The good life can bear good fruit, not only in thoughts and deeds, but especially in good children. The most important crop to care for is the family fruit. The surest way to strengthen the spiritual life is to strengthen the spiritual life of the family. Children, to become creative and co-operative members of the family, need to experience genuine love at home from their early infancy. Newer understanding of physical beginnings makes the serene, believing mother a blessing even before the child is born. She who carries a new life may care for her child's basic spiritual structure more than she thinks by leading a life holy unto the Lord and peaceful for the world.

Children need a constant home environment of genuine love. Pious phrases or forced grins cannot fool them. They know love with their whole being and can separate appearance from reality. When parents abide in God's love day by day both with each other and with the children, that love becomes the source of the child's most basic security. Sham makes children detest the creed the parents profess. Rebellious ministers' children seek the reality of love away from all its false pretenses. Marriage quarrels are bad and sharp words hurt the children, but what really counts is the steady reality of the parents' love for each other and for them.

"Blow-outs" can be forgiven and erased, and do not act as hindrances to renewed community experience on a high level, but lack of love kicks the emotional underpinning from under the child. For the children's sake—and they constitute the coming world—the parents must therefore find love. The test of such love is whether each carries the concerns of the other in his heart, whether he wants to shield his partner from blame or to blame her when something untoward has happened, whether he subordinates his personal desires to the family welfare, and grows to have no desire save the family happiness, or whether he wants what he wants when he wants it, whether he disciplines and eradicates personal faults or rationalizes them into virtues.

Husbands, too, are often made or broken by their family life. Behind successful men often stand women who are themselves emotional successes. They may be of different types. Some may constitute the serene background of emotional stability, symbolizing and enacting spiritual strength. Others may be secure leaders from whom the husbands gather both inspiration and actual guidance. Still others may be constant co-operators in a common venture. In all cases, however, they provide the home life which the husband needs and give him a chance to contribute his best.

To be sure, unmarried men and unhappily married men have often become famous, but the contribution of the well-rounded, naturally-balanced man has within it an unequaled fullness and effectiveness. For the steady welfare of society the world depends upon happily married people.

This is equally true of women. The loving husband, in fact, will want his wife to find life's greatest happiness, whether by letting her have the children she craves, devote herself to family work devoid of straining decisions, co-operate with him in his work, or even find expression in achievements of her own.

Not only for individuals, however, whether children, husbands, or wives, but also for the church the family is the primary unit. Adults can be won more easily for the church through concern for their children than through any other motive. Here is the opportunity of the church, often mentioned but seldom used. Let families be shown concretely spiritual living, therefore, and let the church be concerned with families as such.

The corporate nature of the church and of the family in the church should be maintained as well as discussed. Yet how few families constitute a church at home, and how few worship as families in public. If this cannot be done without disturbing the minister and congregation, something is radically wrong and the worship is faulty. Let reverence and discipline plus hallowed joy incorporate the small family community within the larger local church until both unite intensively and extensively in expressing and fostering the family of God. When that happens within the very fiber of family life the best human material for a better world has united with the fullest divine means. Win the family for the Christian enterprise, then the world is saved.

The family will not be won, however, without an effective approach through the devotional life. We tend to ignore this center of Christian living, as if it would take care of itself. Evil wins by default. We blame our busy schedules. Father must hurry to work. Or mother has to get the children to school. Or brother has his vacation and is entitled to sleep in the morning or to be with his date at night. There is thus no time for family devotions. Others dismiss it as old-fashioned. It is as passé, they feel, as the three-hour sermon.

But family devotions are the most important part of family life. The family altar stands unavoidably at the center of its life, lit and used, or dark and abused. The family is a church by nature, a community under God, either free and outreaching or frustrated and self-concerned. There is always time for what is deemed important. The fault lies not in our lack of time but in our sense of values. What is time for, and how is it to be used by a Christian family if no time is allowed for worship?

The proper time can be found somehow. Families can get up half an hour earlier. Much sleep is wasted by tensions. The worshiping family finds rest and peace in its worship. A new happiness can heal and refresh the weary spirit. So wake the sleepy boy! Shake the drowsy girl! Leave the dishes on the table and the newspaper on the front step and join in duty or in joy the feast of family devotions! Some can do it at night, if the ages of the children permit. Or time can be taken before breakfast or dinner. Special services may be held on Sundays, holidays, or days of celebration. The time is there! Members away from home can read the same passages and pray together in memory, in the divine presence and in anticipation of reunion. Sometimes people may have to have devotions in smaller family sections, through force of circumstance. The Christian family, in any case, lives by family devotions. Strengthen those and you strengthen the family. Win the families and you win the world.

But how is family devotion conducted? If anyone can sing, and if one member can play an instrument, Christian hymns can be sung as a family. We begin our own family devotion each day that way. If each member chooses the hymn of the week, how many hymns soon become the rich background of later life. What a priceless Christian heritage to acquire! Let the baby choose "Jesus Loves Me" and do not tire of the simple words. Sing the adolescent hymns of youth, sharing your young girls' fervor, and live with the sophisticated taste of your college boy. Let the whole family breathe in the beauty of Bach. All must unite in any individual's selection of personal hymns, and no one need suppress his taste for Gospel songs or for hymns of the social gospel as well as for the great affirmations of faith in word and melody. Vigilance is necessary lest such hymn singing degenerates into routine. If the words are not being memorized, they are not being thought while sung.

Use song also as a means of fellowship. How near to your wife you are when you hear her play and sing or when you spend an occasional hour that way. How your boy will be one with you while you sing hymns together. Let the children play their instruments, well or haltingly, and sing with them. Learn to sing as a family in the car. Play alphabet games with Christian songs and make melody with united hearts. Choose theme songs for trips so that all may join reverently in joyful praise or prayer. Or gather around the radio and sing with the programs. Or sit around the fire and sing to the Lord. Stand together in church and hear the young ones let out their voices on the hymns they have learned at home. If at all possible strengthen the spiritual life of the family through song. If the history of a hymn can be obtained, that hymn becomes more meaningful. Some member of the family could make such information a hobby.

Family reading is also of great importance. The Bible should be read each day. We read it in successive portions only when all members living at home are present. It does not take long to get through the New Testament by reading only one paragraph each day in the Revised Standard Version. Sometimes the father will read aloud and all those who can read will follow along in their own Bibles. Sometimes another member will take over. Or sometimes verses may be read in turn. Selected passages from the Old Testament are also suitable for family reading. Much Old Testament material, however, is better covered through readings in the Children's Bible or in books of Old Testament stories, and not as family devotions.

Discussion of what is read should be natural. If discussion is not spontaneous, that shows either too much hurry or not enough interest. Significant comments can be elicited from children. It is advisable to read both King James, for its majestic beauty, and modern translations. If various members have different versions they often pipe up with great excitement when differences of meaning are discovered. Such differences tend to teach youngsters not to take the Bible at too literal a level. One or more commentaries should be handy. Actually the use of commentaries need consume very little time. What can better overcome Biblical illiteracy than such an introduction to the Bible at home as a part of family life?

The family should not, of course, stop with the Bible nor with formal devotional reading. There is good material available in books about the Bible or in selected stories from it. Numerous devotional manuals of real help are available like the *Upper Room*. Our family has profitably read and discussed for years *The Fellowship of Prayer*. Some of the best Advent booklets, like Dwight Bradley's *The Secret Stair*, for example, have enriched our Christmas seasons. Our children found Jones' *The Way to Power and Poise* a bit heavy but profited much by it. It is hard to convey how much joy and instruction we have received from *Pilgrim's Progress, The Eagle Series,* booklets on the lives of missionaries that fascinate the youngsters, and similar standard treasures. There is some biographical and fictional material suitable for family use, but we need much more. No family must ever be so busy or so indifferent that they fail to find the rich rewards awaiting them in this sphere of Christian literature.

Family prayers should be simple and natural. We find kneeling to be generally the best position to assume. When the floor is drafty, however, or when some member of the family does not get dressed on time, common sense must govern the matter of posture. The children catch their parents' attitudes. If they truly pray in the Spirit the children know it. If they do it mostly as a duty the children soon sense that. Then, if ever, the parents need to relax, to recall to whom they are praying and to feel the divine restoration, in order for the family altar to become the joy and power it ought to be.

In our circle we begin by letting the youngest pray first. Children can pray before they can talk. The baby will learn by feeling the emotional warmth of a mother's or father's prayers. He may slip in and out between the parents' knees, but as soon as he begins to talk at all he will join in the amens. It is surprising how soon an infant will participate in the Lord's Prayer with which we end our daily devotions. As soon as he can speak the baby can be taught to pray for the dear ones and to say "Thank you, Father." From then on the child will pray more maturely as he grows, and as he learns from his parents and older brothers and sisters. Very often a child's prayer will be dull and scattered. But that is no shortcoming. That is the way of life. And frequently children will startle their elders by the depths of their insights and by the sterling qualities of their sympathies.

After the youngest child has finished we pray in turn according to age, ending with the father of the family. We do so even when visitors are present. Christians are never embarrassed by their ages. Occasionally one or the other parent may have to recall for the family how important the meeting with God really is and help lift the prayer to a higher level. Most important, however, is the genuineness of the experience of God and the lifting up of the occasion for the Spirit to take charge beyond our faltering speech and wavering attention.

Family prayers, however, are of little worth unless the family has a real sense of family vocation. When the whole family shares day by day in what the breadwinner is doing, not only in conversation about it but in dedication before God, somehow the truth that man cannot live by bread alone becomes vitally apparent. As each child raises to God his parents and their work, a common sense of challenge and of achievement grips the family. In our own family the children put upon me an ever deeper obligation as they keep praying that God may give me the right words to say or to write. When I am away from home, I am never without the assurance of being lifted up in prayer by the family I have left behind. When I face a trying occasion the face of my wife at prayer flashes on my mind, banishing doubt and instilling joy and confidence. God uses the whole family. He promises that the prayers of even two or three for the coming of the Kingdom will be heard. How much, then, can a believing family achieve? Individualism is destroyed, individuals become merged, and social motivation becomes real. We have had children visit us who have prayed with such beauty for their parents' work, that we have actually witnessed how every honest vocation can be felt, enjoyed, and enacted together by a truly praying family.

The basic vocation of the family is not the father's or mother's personal profession. Each family is an intensive unit whose most important job is to be the church, the family of God on a small scale. Each family has as its primary and main task to glorify God and to hasten the coming of His Kingdom. In this calling what each member does, from the oldest to the youngest, is thus of complete importance. Every member of the family must be aware of what each of the others is doing and enter into it with total abandon. Each member lifts up all the others in prayer, remembering their needs, cares, or particular doings for the day. Whenever something significant, good or ill, happens to any member all the others are ready to bear and to share it.

By means of such prayer one's sense of values is altered. Parents do not want their children to shine in school or in the club in order to gratify them. Neither do they want the children to work off their own frustrations. Rather they would have their children be Christian and do their best as Christians above all else. Parents pray that their children may hallow God's name and strive to serve humanity. A narrow competitive spirit is thus broken through and the co-operative attitude takes its place. The family is not pitted against other individuals or families. The parents are concerned that the children be thoughtful of other children's feelings; that they do not make them feel inferior. They want their children to be genuine. The children also know that they are loved for themselves, for what they are, and not because they win prizes and reflect credit on their parents.

Where else can the children learn so well the meaning of the social or co-operative spirit? If the children truly feel that the parents want above all to be good neighbors, that they really want to help and to honor those whom they deal with, the children have already caught such attitudes. Our world is perishing for lack of social motivation. We say that the world could be different if it were not for human nature. We could treat the races differently if only we could eradicate the prejudices which exist. We could have a different economic order if only we could cultivate individual initiative and responsible concern in such a manner that the use of property for the common good would not mean totalitarianism and bureaucracy. We could overcome nationalism if only early juvenile emotions would not block adult perception. We could do away with denominationalism if we could only attain a vision of the common good which yet permits differences of expression. Where, however, can such feelings be learned as well as in the Christian family?

We need a sense of vocation in our work. This is a large undertaking, and the major part of it must be accomplished at home. Let the family find the meaning of its common task around the family altar. What lies outside and beyond consists in letting the domestic hearth reflect and make real God's family of all mankind. When the wholeness of the human race becomes real through the single family and when the real vocation of the latter envisages all society as a community of common concern under a common God, then alone can the family achieve its end and life take on its deepest meaning.

The Christian family can best break down social barriers and cement satisfactory community relations. It can widen the horizons of understanding and co-operation unto the bounds of the world and until the end of time. Win the family effectively for

Christ and you will win the church and the world. Strengthen the spiritual life of the family, in all aspects and dimensions, and you will hasten in the surest way the coming of the Kingdom of God.

IV

Strengthening the Spiritual Life

WE HAVE now considered the divine formula for spiritual success and for personal and family devotions. The spiritual life
does not come easily. It is worth too much for that. It must be
worked at, long and hard. In the present chapter we are to consider some further aspects of the kind of living that bears rich
spiritual fruit when pursued with complete seriousness.

We must consider more fully the matter of reading. Far too
little reading is done to feed the spiritual life, and often this reading is done in the wrong way. Naturally, our first concern is
with the reading of the Bible. When the Bible is read in the
light of the largest logic of God's love, the soul begins to feel its
small walls shake and fall. Unless the Bible provides ever reced-
ing horizons it is being improperly read. The only right way to
read the Bible is to learn how great and good God is, to feel one's
narrowness judged and his lack of faith, and to accept day by day
larger loyalties and aims.

The most important suggestion perhaps is that the Bible be read slowly. Very likely much more is learned from the Bible when two or three verses are pondered each day than when a chapter is skimmed quickly. Pray as the Bible is opened that the heart and mind be prepared to receive and to appropriate. Approach the Bible devotionally. Such an approach does not involve a superstitious awe but a reverent respect. It does not presuppose authority, artificially imposed, that God's truth does not admit our questions. Instead the devotional attitude involves a recognition of the God who speaks in the Bible, of the central importance that the Bible has had for the saints as the standard of their faith, and of all that one's own experience has taught in living with it. The mind should be brought along, however, and not parked outside. One should be as thoughtful as possible of what is read in the Bible, for only thus can one discriminate between its local application and its spiritual meaning for us.

Certainly if the Christ had to come to us in the weaknesses of the flesh, must not likewise the record of Him be clothed in the weaknesses of a book? This does not deny but insures the authoritative character of the Bible, because such is God's way of manifesting Himself in the world. An open heart and an open mind, seeking in faith God's truth for the world, will, as a result of keeping open, find the milk and the meat of the Gospels. Besides lengthy reading for information, small passages must be perused, preferably in succession, and thoroughly digested until they are assimilated as the subconscious background of thought. The spiritual life cannot be valid if we read the newspaper more leisurely and readily than the good news of God.

In the second place, one ought to find a few minutes each day to dwell with the great saints of the Church. Let me be frank in admitting that my own life suffers when I do not feed it on wise devotional reading as well as when I do not pray with some who know intimately the life of prayer. Those whose writings have helped me the most are Fénelon, De Sales, à Kempis and Oldham. Fénelon, that wondrously wise spiritual guide, can be read in two American translations, *Christian Perfection* and *Spiritual Letters*. De Sales' *The Devout Life* and à Kempis' *The Imitation of Christ* are well known. The book which I have used the most has been Oldham's *Devotional Diary*. For many years I have gone over and over it both by myself and with my classes. Baillie's *A Diary of Private Prayer*, Gore's *The Lord's Prayer*, Vernier's *Not as the World Giveth*, Clark's *I Will Lift Up Mine Eyes*, Heard's *Prayers and Meditations*, Bunyan's *Grace Abounding*, Munro's *Truth for Today*, Huegel's *Fairest Flower*, Boehme's *The Way to Christ*, Kierkegaard's *Edifying Discourses* and *Christian Discourses*, Phillips' *The Choice Is Always Ours*, Blakney's *Meister Eckhart* are titles taken almost at random which I have ingested slowly, savoring their wisdom day by day. When I fail to seek such nurture I feel a hunger and a weakness which I know are real.

Such reading need not consume much time, but it must be done slowly, steadily, and thoughtfully. To become practitioners of the spiritual life we must live with the masters and profit from them. One word of caution is necessary, not to indulge your own taste exclusively. Live day by day with both spiritual radicals and conservatives. Read Augustine, *The Prayer Book* (Episcopal), Fox, Wesley, and Woolman, and modern devotional writers of all creeds and persuasion.

For my part, I feel a genuine lack of devotional reading from great non-Christian souls. How else can we learn to know these

religions intimately unless we live with them slowly and as far
as possible profoundly? I have been surprised at the depth and
devotional character of the best in Bahai scriptures as presented,
for instance, in Townshend's *The Promise of All Ages.* Can
truth hurt us if we serve her with all our heart, or can its universal speech separate us from the love of God in Christ Jesus our
Lord? Let us not repudiate any means of growth. But let us also
hold fast our original and primary guides, pre-eminently the
Bible.

The third kind of reading that should be done to strengthen
the spiritual life might be called study. The mind must be well
exercised if it is to be fit to serve the well-being of the whole
person. The spirit needs the new light which the mind can bring
it. Growth depends partly on hard study. For the development of
the devotional life books like Whiston's *Teach Us to Pray,* But-
trick's *Prayer,* or Harkness' *Prayer and the Common Life* ought
to be studied carefully for content. Undiluted theology also should
be grappled with. Theology deals with problems which perplex
the self and stunt its growth. Every person should seek out the
theology that answers his questions as to the why of things,
the problem of evil, the ways of providence, the nature and
destiny of life. But study comes second, not first. First in order
are worship and prayer. But real advance raises many questions
for the intellect, though the process of growth also produces the
answers to those questions. Thus we can learn from those who
have faced these perplexities and found an answer that really
satisfies.

Watch out for easy answers that are not as complex as the
problems of life. They are short cuts and substitutes to avoid. The
true answers are both as simple as the saint makes them and as

complex as the world in which he lives. Watch out, too, for comforting answers that demand little of the asker. They are the theologies of the false prophets that have no real Gospel. The truth is as satisfying as the all-dependable and all-concerned love of God but also as hard as the Cross He offers the self both to die on and from which to derive new, wondrous life. Find the theology that answers your intellectual needs to see for yourself, that demands everything of you, and that leaves you still restless for the fuller truth and the better life. No other theology is good enough or true enough. Without real satisfaction of mind, however, there can be no genuine well-being for the soul. Without peace of mind there cannot be peace of soul.

You also need stimulus to keep going. Get yourself a partner with whom to discuss what you have read. Organize a study group to wrestle with the Bible or with theology. Get yourself a prayer partner too. Such a partnership may endure for years. Or it may last only for a number of months and then a new one may be formed. During the years I have had a number of people who have prayed with me more or less regularly and have helped me more than they were aware of. Do not, however, become dependent upon them. Learn to pray in the closet more and more, even while you cultivate the companionship of the two or three. You may never know how much you need someone else to share your experience before you have tried such sharing. The selection of a partner or partners must be more or less obvious and natural. Spiritual companionship cannot be forced. Open the door of your life and let God and others do the rest as far as the solution of this need goes.

You may find a prayer group which you may join. Lose yourself in it. Often ministers are too self-conscious and are too much used to the prima donna role to get a group really going. That is the very reason, however, that they must succeed here, or know that they have failed to bear the fruits of faith. The new life will come largely through prayer. The new world will also come largely through prayer. It will come bit by bit as more and more learn to be genuine in their quiet and constant seeking to know God and to do His will. Thus housewives, farmers, railroad porters, businessmen find the occasion to sustain radiant prayer groups.

Never try to force group solidarity or complain about its failures. Examine, rather, your own life and provide more power for fellowship within your own prayers. Often I despair, for instance, about the possibility of real prayer among seminary faculties and students. Yet some of my holiest memories are from such bending before God in seminaries to share each other's problems and joys. Keep on believing and waiting and see if creativity does not blossom around you wherever you are. When people pray believingly things happen more than appears on the surface. However halting and sporadic, perhaps even occasional, be such a prayer group, thank God for it and take courage to use better whatever door is opened to you.

Certainly we have failed the churches at this point. The prayer meeting has generally died by default. Perhaps it had to die. Modern education, particularly the general interest in popular psychology, has dampened people's desire to reveal their inner selves. If anything, however, ought to help us to have better prayer meetings it should be the knowledge of psychology. We can now understand ourselves better and use this very psychology to test the spirits. The prayers and testimonies which center in the will of God and the common good have nothing to fear from psychology. The lives that long for nothing except to be rid of the drives which hurt the self and others need have no fear of being understood. They witness not to their own goodness but to the sufficiency of God's grace. We have grown afraid of one another, of strangers within the walls of the church, which walls divide the lives of us all. What we need is to be set free from these barriers.

Personally, I can think of no place I want to be known so well as on my knees confessing my own sins and faults and finding the strength and forgiveness to start again. I know no way to find fellowship so real and so lasting as within circles of prayer. We need more wisdom to conduct prayer meetings. Above all we need the spiritual fire to have them correspond to reality within the participants. Religion becomes a sham unless we ourselves are constrained by it, and we never shall be until we pray as individuals, families, groups, and churches.

All the prayer and study in the world, however, will never make God real or change our lives unless we live so that our "prayers be not hindered." As individuals and as families we must examine our lives in the light of the Gospel, submit to being judged by it, and be enabled by it to achieve lives full of healing and help. Over and over again we fail. Such is the way of all true growth in freedom. But through all failures of dedicated spirits runs a line of growing reality, transformed attitudes, and effective action. God never fails us if we trust Him for a new kind of life.

There are some definite rules, moreover, for real Christian living. First of all we must surrender our whole selves to God, both their conscious and the subconscious constituents. This takes time. A very prominent professor in one of our seminaries confessed that after four hours of trying to find full surrender, a few spiritual leaders became very much discouraged. They were still not much different in their feelings and thoughts. Total surrender takes at least a lifetime. When our present self finds surrender, moreover, God lets us have ever larger selves to surrender! Certainly Jesus had to keep surrendering to the end, through Gethsemane and Calvary. The saints know what years of self-offering are involved. As one area is won they have found that God lets us find another to be used for him. Spiritual pain and sense of failure must be no source of worry, for guilt feelings always accompany the growing life. When God declares present attainment inadequate His judgment makes us feel guilty about it; but how else could we ever keep growing? Be concerned, rather, if you feel that your life has attained its fulfillment. Especially be concerned if you suspect that you are a saint. Surrender is the hardest thing life offers and uses up all the time we have. Surrender is the ever present door to Christian living.

Surrender, however, is not negative but positive. We should, perhaps, instead of surrender, call it the constant acceptance of God's gracious will. Surrender, however, is the opening of the door which God will not break down. Surrender is our job. Our surrender is made to God who gives us freely all things. We surrender the narrow, shut-in self to find the wide-seeing and free self. We surrender the self that is feverishly and vainly set on its own way to find God's life-satisfying way. We surrender the self that nourishes its own hurts and prejudices to find the self of fellowship which rejoices in other people's joy and finds redemptive gladness in helping their hurts. Surrender is the door, the abundant life beyond it is the heart of the Christian faith.

Surrender becomes cheap and evasive, nevertheless, when it is merely or mostly an emotional formula for feeling secure with God. Real security does not come about that way, for God is no dispenser of comforts to pious prigs. Surrender to God means genuineness of life, first of all. It is self-acceptance. It is seeing oneself as one is, in need of being remade. It is no longer feeling sorry for the self but finding faith to remold that self for the common good. Always and ever the Christian life is tested by its fruits. Does the person become more outgoing and less self-involved, not in talk and sermon but in actual deeds? Does he become more thoughtful of others? Does he become more willing to accept blame and less willing to criticize? Does he become more disciplined and less self-indulgent? Does his horizon grow and his concrete concerns expand from self and family, to neighbors and community, to the church and the Church Universal, to the nation and the world? Does he accept responsibility and do things, or does he find fault and make excuses?

Christianity is not worth the breath it takes to say the creed unless it can produce individuals who have found in concrete living a new community commitment in every dimension. A rabid sectarian, a racialist, a sectionalist, a nationalist shows by his fruits that his heart is full of something that is not Christianity. In Christ there is no overagainstness but a complete concern for all. Christ is the love incarnate that casts out fear. Most of our thinking is based on fear. It is defensive. We see criticism in what people say. We find bad news most interesting because we ourselves live in fear. We build theologies of fear in the name of the dispeller of fear.

As sure as Christ is Christ a real Christian breaks down barriers among groups at home, among the churches, in the communities, and to the ends of the earth. Unless a Christian has his whole life set on the making of effective peace, positive and creative, his is a vain confession. The Christian makes grace abound or he is no channel for the Christ. New attitudes and new actions are always involved in the genuine article which is the Christian faith.

Particularly important is the matter of giving. The Christian first of all gives his whole life and all that he is and has. He has to struggle to keep back what he is saving to provide for the future security of his family or for other responsibilities. The Christian rejoices in giving. Perhaps it is wise to set aside in prayer some such sum as 10 per cent of one's wages for Christian purposes.

I do not mean to devise any legalistic formula, but unless there is some regular way of giving, much energy is lost in deciding about each particular occasion. Find out what satisfies your heart in God's sight, and then give it joyously. One must not keep giving because of guilt feelings. Never grieve over giving what you have decided upon *before God* when you happen to be short of money, nor grieve because you have no more to give. God has ample physical means. What He needs is for you to give in faith and as a dedicated answer to His voice in your heart. Perhaps you may be counted on to give more during some particular occasion. During the war many young couples perhaps felt called upon to give more than seemed wise at the time, but in retrospect they see that everything worked out well. Certainly if you do not like to give you know well indeed where your heart is not.

The amount is not what counts the most, though we obviously must be careful not to delude ourselves on this score. What counts the most is what we give, how we give, and why we give. We all want to give to the church to bless it and make it a blessing. Let the church of God be ever well supplied. But ever as Christians let us give to good community and secular causes. Let us give where actual need is effectually met with as little overhead expense as possible.

We should give quietly and perhaps scatter our gifts rather widely so as not to become too important to any organization. Some causes we support regularly; others as the spirit moves us. There may be so many calls on our pocketbook that we cannot contribute to all. One saint I know answers every appeal, and he has many, even if with only a dollar. He gives and gives never despairing. Others have to say no and focus their response at least to some extent. No rule can be set except that we ought to give to organizations that cover the full gamut of spirit, mind, and body. Let the whole man be served. This means that some organizations will be definitely spiritual in their aid, others educational, and still others will render mostly physical services. Particularly important for Christians is, of course, to give wisely to unpopular causes, where fears and narrow pressures prevent most people from giving at all. Need I mention that our dependants near and dear are a primary obligation, as Jesus himself pointed out?

Giving should be both wise and dedicated. Preferably the whole family should participate in it. Children learn to give and to worship through giving. Children should know where the gifts go, and even how and why. If a certain sum represents the regular family giving, special love offerings should be made besides, at Thanksgiving and at Christmas, perhaps when God blesses the family unexpectedly, or when hearts feel particularly thankful. Perhaps a child will pray for someone to whom you used to send CARE packages. Let yourself be moved to match that prayer of concern with a new package *that very day* and let the whole family thank God for the privilege. Much giving has to be impersonal, but occasionally give something special like a goat to Japan or send packages to some saint abroad who is not exactly starving, but whom God wants to bless by being remembered. The wife may feel strongly about some cause of her own. Let her have money for her use. The husband may have his own reasons for some private giving. Let him do so in secret. Much blessing, growth, and joy is definitely lost because our lives are not genuine channels of love.

Above all, give in prayer and thanksgiving. Present the check at the family altar. Take the pledge card to the prayer circle. There is a difference between a cup of cold water and giving it in Christ's name. The difference is no superstition but hard fact. When we give in Christ's name we give gratefully to God and for the common good as privileged instruments. No sense of superiority is to be taken from Christian giving, only the joy of being counted unworthy servants. But unworthy servants may be accepted as actually friends and sons of God!

To strengthen the spiritual life we must use the "divine formula:" Worship, work, wait. We shall never improve personal or family devotions apart from these three means of strengthening the spiritual life. Only as we worship God can we work for Him to the fullest advantage, guided and constrained by His inclusive concern. Only as we work genuinely for the common good can we feel the need for the worship where the whole self cries for God to help us with our puny efforts to make His reality known and to make a better world. Only as we wait can we learn that growth does not depend upon us but upon Him who gives the increase, we know not how.

Pray we must, study we must, give we must; but above all we must find our lives bathed in the reality of God's faithfulness. As we worship, work, and wait, we shall become surprised that, as God becomes more and more real, we may come to feel ourselves less and less worthy and able. But others will find strength and help from us and tell how serenity and strength increasingly characterize our spiritual life. All of life's values will become steadily changed. Though we cannot ourselves understand why and how, the fever of life is over, and we experience a healing and well-being beyond our deserts.